Green Guide to the Architect's Job Book

Second edition

Sandy Halliday

RIBA ### Publishing

© Sandy Halliday, 2000, 2007

Published by RIBA Publishing, 15 Bonhill Street, London EC2P 2EA

1st edition published 2000

ISBN 978 1 85946 186 0

Stock Code 55696

British Library Cataloguing-in-Publication Data
A catalogue record for this book is available from the British Library.

Publisher: Steven Cross
Commissioning Matthew Thompson
Project Editor: Alasdair Deas
Cover design: Philip Handley
Printed and bound by MPG Books, Bodmin, Cornwall

Photographs
Sandy Halliday (front cover, pages 1, 19, 23, 41, 51, 54, 66, 70); Michael Wolshover/ Gaia Architects (pages 15, 57, 63); Howard Liddell (page 32); Ian Cameron (page 48).

RIBA Publishing is part of RIBA Enterprises Ltd.
www.ribaenterprises.com

Contents

Acknowledgements

Thanks are due to those who kindly commented on this second edition and on earlier drafts, especially to all at Gaia Architects, Edinburgh. I would also like to thank Matthew Thompson at RIBA Enterprises for his support, and his enthusiasm to pursue a second edition.

Particular thanks must go to Howard Liddell. Howard is sustainability spokesperson for the Royal Incorporation of Architects in Scotland (RIAS), and his practical achievements in implementing sustainable design in practice have recently been acknowledged with the first and currently only A* rating in the RIAS Sustainable Design Accreditation Scheme. His buildings are an inspiration and his experience of professional practice, ecological design, community consultation and architectural education has been a crucial source of guidance.

Introduction

Not a Luxury Issue

This publication is designed to sit alongside the *Architect's Job Book* so that busy professionals can include sustainable development considerations as part of their remit. It is intended to provide information on crucial factors at each Work Stage of the Plan of Work, which will assist delivery of more sustainable buildings. The first edition of the *Architect's Job Book* was published in 1969 in response to 'the perceived need to complement architectural flair and imagination with a systematic approach to the design and construction process'. Its stated aim was 'to assist architects to translate design into a finished building within time and cost constraints'.

The past four decades have seen many changes to building technology, forms of contract and procurement methods and, importantly, to the way that the impact of buildings and the built environment are perceived. Contractual, technological and procurement changes have been addressed by subsequent editions of the *Job Book*, and in these respects it maintains its applicability to any building and procurement method. Consequently, it continues to fulfil its purpose and remains an essential aide-memoire for practising architects and for students, independent of architectural style. However, notable by their absence are any changes to reflect the shift in awareness of the impact of the built environment and construction processes on the natural environment, and on individuals, communities and organisations, save to the extent that this is necessitated by legislation.

In 1992 the UK Government made a commitment to seek sustainable development strategies, and it has followed through with policy and guidance on sustainable construction and sustainable communities. Central and local government have also introduced a range of economic interventions, such as the carbon levy, landfill tax and congestion charging, aimed at reversing unsustainable trends in a range of sectors. Progress has been made on the development of regulations, codes and indicators. A number of local authorities and clients are setting benchmark standards for buildings beyond, or in addition to, regulation as part of their procurement strategies, although these are not always the most sensible, cost-effective or environmentally effective options available.

As a consequence, the construction industry is developing policies and practices that can lead to built development projects that are, simultaneously, more efficient in the use of resources, less prone to economic penalties, much more socially accountable, more attentive to the quality of design of buildings and the spaces between buildings and much less damaging to the environment than before – that is, '**more sustainable construction**'. These factors really are transforming procurement and design in practice and will do so increasingly as environmental feedback, science, ethics, legislation and the needs of clients and users increasingly oblige us to consider sustainability issues as a positive driver of the right kind of high-quality development in the right place.

Clearly, sustainable design is neither the luxury issue nor the optional extra it has too often been perceived as being. It is therefore timely that architects' responsibilities in creating a sustainable built environment are acknowledged and this aspect of professional practice embraced. There is a lot of confusion around this subject: semantic, intellectual and technical. Much of the confusion results from misunderstanding about '**sustainability**'.

There is a lot of evidence – in poetry, crafts and art – that humankind is deeply connected to the environment, but sustainability is fundamentally different. It is about 'how do we develop?' Its emergence as a concept results from the focusing of ideas that has brought about a broad understanding that it is necessary and possible to implement checks and balances in pursuit of genuine sustained progress for all.

This supplementary guide – now in its second edition – therefore aims simply, but importantly, to support and contemporise the *Job Book* by introducing its readership to the process aspects of sustainable design and to the management of sustainable design practice.

The sections of this guide are intended to aid the process of delivery of sustainable buildings based on the assertion that intervention at any point of the process can have a beneficial outcome. However, adopting the principles at the earliest possible stage in the design process, and maintaining vigilance through to handover and beyond, offers the best chance of delivering a truly sustainable outcome.

In keeping with the 'cradle-to-cradle' approach of sustainable design, this guide includes two additional stages in the building life cycle that are not in the RIBA Outline Plan of Work; these are M: Refurbishment and N: Demolition. This was a convention begun in the early 1990s with the development of the ***Environmental Code of Practice for Buildings and their Services***. Special attention has also been given to the phase of discussion that occurs before any formal agreements are signed.

Additional valuable sources of practical guidance are given in the references section at the end of this guide, which also includes details of those in publications referred to in ***bold italic*** in the body of the text.

Why a Green Guide?

Until recently, sustainable building design was seen as a peripheral activity, largely outside the expressed role of conventional professional practice, and even very recently described by the profession as 'a moral stick with which to bash one's colleagues'. To many it has been unworthy of much attention and often naively perceived as a style or trend to be resisted. However, it is increasingly evident that it is not a trend, or a stick, but an approach that requires systematic care. It requires designing to take full account of quality-of-life issues, resources and the natural environment, to which we must all ultimately defer. This guide is a response to the need for all building design to be more responsive to the environment and more accountable to society.

Designers and specifiers can take steps to make a difference in areas under their influence. For many this involves the application of a set of design parameters with which they might be unfamiliar, or give less than full attention in many circumstances. There are aspects that are relevant throughout the design and procurement process, and because sustainable design is a process not an act this includes a requirement to think beyond handover to the building(s) in use and beyond. The intended outcome is buildings that are less damaging to the natural environment, and are more responsive to their owners' and users' needs.

What's in a Name?

The title of 'Green Guide' deserves explanation.

At the time of writing the first edition, in 1999, many commentators would have preferred it to be a 'sustainable development' or 'sustainable construction' guide. Then, as now, the term 'sustainable' was widely abused and too often used where energy studies or resource management would have been adequate, and indeed more accurate. It seemed unseemly and irresponsible to jump on the bandwagon.

Also, at that time few things within the scope of the majority of architectural decision-making could make a real contribution to sustainability because in general we lacked the appropriate cultural and infrastructural framework to recognise it and underpin it. There were few people really seeking to deliver sustainable design, and thankfully fewer still claiming to have achieved it. 'Green' was considered to be the most appropriate overarching term to describe a process of seeking improvement and to best communicate the content and the opportunities offered to most architects by use of the guide. The 'S-word' was therefore used strictly and specifically.

Seven years has made a difference. The three contributory elements of sustainable development – community welfare, economic sufficiency and environmental enhancement – are significantly better understood. Policies are in place. The Government is addressing the need for an indicator of **development** which is attuned to people's aspirations beyond gross national product (the usual measure of growth). The impact (positive and negative) of the built environment on people's lives is increasingly acknowledged, and so is the role of good design in enhancing the positive impact. There is a wealth of literature on the subject.

In Scotland, primary legislation, the *Building (Scotland) Act 2003,* makes provision for ministers to make building regulations for the purpose of *furthering sustainable development*. The Architects Registration Board (ARB), the Royal Institute of British Architects (RIBA) and the Royal Incorporation of Architects in Scotland (RIAS) have agreed that an understanding of sustainability is a validation requirement in architectural education. The Royal Academy of Engineering has made understanding sustainable design a core competence in engineering education.

The RIAS runs an evidence-based accreditation scheme to provide third-party acknowledgement of architects' achievements in sustainable building design. There is a requirement for all professionals to become competent in the issues, and an enthusiasm by clients to do the same, either directly or through using specialist advice. Therefore, architects are now well placed to make a significant contribution to sustainable development. The original title of 'Green Guide' has therefore been preserved only for continuity, but with affection.

How Will This Guide Help?

What follows is intended to assist practising architects to try, as far as possible, to ensure that all new buildings, and the refurbishment or demolition of existing buildings, is undertaken with a view to enhancing long-term benefits and minimising long-term liabilities.

It should, like the *Architect's Job Book*, be a positive contribution to 'complement architectural flair and imagination with a systematic approach to the design and construction process' and, to paraphrase the *Job Book*, to assist architects to translate design into a finished building within time, cost and environmental constraints.

When used with the appropriate procurement method it should assist in providing a framework for:

- Establishing, developing and communicating client priorities and value systems;

- Setting the sustainable development strategy, and meeting appropriate targets;

- Maintaining the strategy throughout the project;

- Engaging with stakeholders;

- Selecting the design and delivery team;

- Identifying the need for specialist advice;

- Setting appropriate fee structures;

- Developing teamwork and robust communication;

- Facilitating interdisciplinary design;

- Improving briefing procedures;

- Improving user and management participation at an early stage in the design process;

- Developing engineered solutions involving passive design and good ergonomic control;

- Establishing construction and post-construction integrity testing, and making it contractual;

- Preparing tender documentation such that sustainability issues are tied down, and not optional extras;

- Ensuring assessment of the environmental quality of materials and products;

- Reducing waste throughout the life cycle, including designing for deconstruction and recycling;

- Minimising use of toxic substances;

- Encouraging fail-safe innovation of products, systems and processes;

- Establishing supply chain management where specifications involve real or perceived innovation;

- Implementing environmentally and socially responsible site procedures;

- Ensuring that handover is undertaken properly;

- Establishing and then implementing formal feedback mechanisms.

The Role of Clients

The role of clients should not be forgotten and this guide is intended as much for clients as for design teams; their role is crucial. Much of the effect of this guide will be lost if clients and project managers are not involved and motivated. To this end, this publication puts great emphasis on client involvement.

Clients must be encouraged to consider the environmental, economic and social impacts of their buildings and confront their responsibilities as ethical consumers, as well as their moral and legal obligations and rights. It is not sufficient to simply delegate responsibilities to project managers.

Clients are being presented with choices in procurement. Their increased understanding about long-term costs and impacts means that many are actively seeking sustainable buildings. However, to achieve the right result they do need to recognise the real practicalities of buildings. They need to select the right teams – teams with a genuine commitment to delivering sustainable buildings and the skills to do so – if necessary through partnering or specialist advisors. Sustainability must be recognised as the responsibility of all involved and not an isolated issue. Communities and users that are likely to be affected by a project should be fully engaged and, where possible, involved in decision-making and long-term management.

The tendency for clients to think that sustainable design is primarily concerned with adding on expensive elements such as photovoltaic panels or geothermal heat pumps is not helpful. It is important to start from a premise that current design approaches are not optimised and to seek to build from a base of conservation and quality in design and construction in order to spend money more wisely.

There is significant evidence that investment in design can reduce costs and environmental impact, so training or specialist advisory services should be considered at stages throughout the process. Looking at economic impact over a longer timescale than commonly applied will deliver cost-in-use savings and significantly reduce adverse impacts by providing increased choice to designers seeking sustainable solutions.

Finally, clients and design teams need to set strict and auditable targets using good third-party assessment tools, which contribute to the process of continual improvement. Ultimately it isn't awards that count, it's the performance – for owners, managers, users, accountants and the environment. All the people involved need to commit themselves, and appropriate resources, to feedback and to appreciate that buildings need a planned handover period and good management in order to work well in the long term.

Key Principles

This guide does not seek to be a primer on sustainability issues, but it does provide an opportunity to highlight the ways, and extent to which, buildings impact on the environment, the individuals and the communities that they are intended to support. Buildings and the built environment will increasingly be required to satisfy six key criteria:

- Enhance biodiversity;

- Support communities;

- Use resources effectively;

- Minimise pollution;

- Create healthy environments;

- Manage to process.

In order to achieve this there is a fundamental requirement for the construction process to be appropriately managed using a combination of new skills, tools and techniques, which are discussed below.

There is a great deal that is new to learn. However, the transition to a culture of more sustainable construction can be based on a positive agenda. This involves an appreciation of our environment, and the aspiration to maintain and enhance it through appropriate architecture that fully meets the needs of individuals and communities. This publication, like the *Job Book*, seeks to provide knowledge of these issues, the appropriate questions to ask and, importantly, the proper time to ask them.

Success will rely on understanding the issues and their relevance and then identifying the best sources of practical guidance. Shared commitments and positive relationships with the client or client group, within a design team, and between a design team and a contractor are more likely to have a beneficial impact than prescriptive approaches; albeit these may be necessary in the short term. Commitment by all involved and firm agreement of responsibilities at an early stage, for example, are likely to be significant components of success.

Enhance Biodiversity

The majority of construction activity transforms natural habitats into environments where species other than humans struggle to exist. Consideration of natural habitats and breeding patterns during construction is a requirement of best practice construction management schemes (such as the Considerate Constructors Scheme and CEEQUAL – the Civil Engineering Environmental Quality Assessment and Award Scheme), as is monitoring of changes in biodiversity.

Design of buildings, landscape and the public realm, if undertaken with sensitivity, can enhance opportunities for species' colonisation through provision of wildlife corridors, use of surface water, native planting, designed breeding areas and avoidance of polluting treatments and materials. Central and local government have biodiversity plans and aspirations – aiming to protect and enhance existing biodiversity – and the built environment needs to be integrated with these. There are numerous good examples.

Support Communities

The built environment has a crucial impact on the physical and economic health and well-being of individuals, communities and organisations. Where buildings contribute to ill-health (through poor ventilation and moisture management or use of chemical toxins) and alienation (through poor transport facilities and access to amenities); undermine community (through poor private and public space provision) and create excessive financial liability (through inefficiency), they are undesirable and unsustainable. Interventions are needed that identify and meet the needs and requirements of communities and contribute to enhancing community aspirations. This may be a defined geographical community or a business community. The higher the level of real community involvement the more successful a development is likely to be, and there is a need to find inventive ways to cultivate a 'real' involvement in order to overcome a slide towards consultation fatigue. The issues at stake are:

- Choice – particularly, but not solely, for the most disadvantaged;

- Affordability – particularly where this means lowering standards from an already inadequate level and creating excessive long-term liability;

- Identity – to create a sense of place and to overcome the blandness and sameness of much contemporary development;

- Satisfaction – through designed private and public spaces, mixed-use development, local services and social infrastructure, including good transport choices.

Use Resources Effectively

Buildings and infrastructure represent a significant use of human, economic and environmental resources. Building, and extraction of fossil fuels and materials to fuel the industry, changes the landscape, natural habitats and ecosystems, and causes damage and irreversible depletion.

Conserving resources (land, money, energy, water, human) is invariably good value in the long term. At its best this can lead to imaginative solutions, rather than simply presuming an infinite supply of goods, services and resources. Demand-side management should take precedence, and the emphasis should be on minimising the natural resources required in the first place.

Transport, with its significant consumption of energy resources and its impact on how people use space, is vitally important and is influenced by planning policies, particularly in relation to mixed-use development and the design of the public realm which affect the need to travel. An integrated approach to transport within the framework of this guide could contribute many small steps towards an overall improvement in the urban and rural infrastructure.

Minimise Pollution

Few industries that supply the construction sector derive from, or deliver, 'clean' products or technologies. The majority of materials and products are chemically and mechanically transformed, and some contain significant industrial pollution, including re-engineered waste, which may have limited life and then no further use. The construction industry, and the industries that support it, are major contributors to a persistent poisoning of the natural and the man-made environment. This poisoning is apparent:

- In the global atmosphere, by the depletion of the ozone layer and climate change;

- On land, by the pollution of soil and water courses by industrial and agricultural wastes and runoff from roads;

- At sea, by increasing levels of toxins in sea birds and sea mammals derived from human and chemical waste;

- Inside buildings, by the entrapment of moisture and inadequate ventilation, and by increasing levels of synthetic chemicals from construction, cleaning and maintenance activities, contributing to the occurrence of building-related ill-health;

- Internally to humans, by dramatic increases in random occurrences of cancers, and by the acknowledged impact of the indoor environment on allergies and asthma.

Create Healthy Environments

The *Construction (Design and Management) Regulations 1994* (CDM, updated in 2007) had a huge impact on site hazards and on health and safety procedures. However, a sustainable approach recognises the issues of pollution (described above) as legitimate health and safety concerns and seeks to integrate a mitigation strategy into the design process. It is important that everyone involved in the construction process recognises the potentially hazardous effects of buildings and construction processes – which go far beyond the occasional construction or domestic accident or avoidable error. The problem of buildings-related ill-health is far more endemic. The outcome of the design process should ensure that buildings have a positive impact on health and well-being rather than simply minimising negative aspects. Architectural quality is essential. This means that designers must give due attention to materials specification to avoid known and suspected buildings-related toxins and allergens, and to minimise the conditions in which they can have an adverse impact. Daylight makes a vital contribution to people's experience and well-being inside buildings, and moisture management is essential to prevent the development of unhealthy environments and harmful organisms.

Manage the Process

There is increasing recognition of the need for process guidance to support specialist management of the design and construction process in order to take aspirations reliably through to successful delivery and beyond – into genuine long-term sustainability.

It is a considerable step forward that sustainable buildings are beginning to be recognised as part of a process, rather than simply a product at handover. This guide is intended to be a significant contribution to this aspect, but there is a wide range of additional tools and techniques available to assist clients or design teams to deliver sustainable design and to appraise the degree to which objectives are being met.

The techniques vary from those that seek to establish sustainable construction as a process conforming to real limitations on resources and impact, to checklists that encourage issues to be considered. Tools exist for appraisal of materials, resources, products, places, components, buildings, professional practice, processes, social factors, and business performance and investment. Issues covered include design quality, place, biodiversity, occupant satisfaction, transport, indoor air quality, light quality and quantity, energy/water/land use and cost, emissions, noise, waste, volatile organic compounds (VOCs), embodied energy, embodied toxicity and more.

Architects reading this guide may wish to consider undertaking specialist continuing professional development (CPD) or registering under the Sustainable Architecture Scheme run by RIAS. Other designers may wish to promote similar schemes through their own professional bodies so that their achievements can be acknowledged. Clients may wish to look to current lists of designers registered under such schemes.

Before you start...

The period of discussion that occurs before any formal agreements are signed, and so before the start of the Outline Plan of Work, is the opportunity to ensure that everyone who is going to be involved understands the nature of a sustainable approach, together with the benefits, responsibilities and issues.

Whatever the nature and scope of the professional services provided, some principles and good practice procedures will always be applicable.

Commitment

The first step in the process of achieving a sustainable project is to secure the necessary commitment on the part of the client and/or those with the requisite authority within the client group. This may take the form of a Sustainable Development/Environmental Policy or Statement by the client, or the adoption of a formal environmental management system or environmental assessment method(s) as a way of benchmarking proposals. Alternatively, or in addition, this may be expressed through the development of an appropriate brief with clear targets. Achieving the commitment may require the client group to undergo some form of induction on sustainability issues. Responsibilities for ensuring the agreed targets should be clearly assigned.

Degrees of Green

The manner in which the sustainability agenda is introduced and any priority issues are likely to depend on knowledge of the client, the prospective users, the method of procurement and other pertinent issues.

The degree of client commitment will have a bearing on the extent to which they are likely to accept more innovative design solutions. Too little consideration of sustainability could have a negative impact on the project outcome because the opportunities and benefits offered by a sustainable approach are likely to become increasingly apparent. Hence it is essential to have knowledgeable inputs at the outset in order confirm the aims at the briefing stage (see table on pages 26–27). Sustainable solutions should be neither more expensive nor more complicated than less benign alternatives but should focus in the first instance on basic quality in design and construction. However, good quality design and construction cannot under any circumstance compete financially with poor quality.

Benefits to Clients

If possible involve the client in a thorough discussion of the issues and the legal and other responsibilities that might inform their approach. It may be an appropriate time to discuss the client's operational as well as building needs, and to introduce them to issues of which they may be unaware. It is a good idea to draw attention to direct opportunities and benefits such as cost-in-use, user satisfaction, community enhancement, improved health and productivity and reduced liability. It will help clients (and design team members) to visit a range of projects with similar and relevant objectives, including examples of best practice, and to meet with those involved.

Cost

Cost remains the primary aspect of discussion on sustainable building. Most people involved with construction activities hold the view that sustainable design costs more or is less profitable. It appears self-evident. If it were cheaper or more profitable then in market-driven economies everyone would be doing it.

However, in truth very little is really known about costs, and few people who support the idea that sustainable design costs more or is less profitable have any idea how much more, or how much less profitable. The best available data indicate no discernable statistical relationship between capital costs of similar types of buildings and their environmental impact (see Halliday S.P. *Sustainable Construction*). We do know that many beneficial features have little or no additional capital cost but deliver cost benefits in use. German and American research indicates that increasing design time to integrate sustainability at the outset tends to save on capital and running costs, while late considerations tend to increase costs significantly.

Importantly, the sustainability agenda requires policy to be directed to reversing unsustainable trends and the impact of this is likely to be a rapid increase in costs of unsustainable and wasteful practice, making today's decisions even more important financially.

Professional Responsibilities

The form of appointment may be something on which an architect will be asked to advise. For example, they might communicate to the client the importance of vigilance in respect of sustainability matters at all Work Stages if the project is to have a successful outcome. Considering the ability of all team members to integrate and control environmental considerations may have an influence on the various types of appointment, the associated roles and responsibilities, and any specialist consultants and/or requirements.

It will be useful to be aware of the sustainable development policies and practices of companies, and also the policies endorsed by architecture's professional bodies, such as RIBA and RIAS, and by those of other members of the design team as they are appointed (CIBSE, RICS, IStructE, ICE and so on).

When appointing building services engineering specialists, it may be beneficial to consider using fee scales that are related to benchmarks of building performance to encourage environmentally engineered solutions, instead of the widespread practice of linking fees to equipment cost. Insist also on a post-occupancy involvement.

Crucially, the design team members must demonstrate an understanding of the significance of pursuing a sustainable design strategy; and they should have the appropriate skills and commitment to the objectives. Given the widespread misunderstanding and confusion, some induction related to best practice development and targets may be valuable.

A: Appraisal

Work Stage A is the opportunity to take a project from an intention, through a commitment to proceed, to development of a brief for a feasibility study. Consideration of environmental and social impacts must be integral from the earliest point. This is the opportunity to establish the level of commitment from all concerned, to involve all those who can contribute to a successful project, and to establish the appropriate procedures, emphasis and priorities to take the project forward.

It will be useful at this stage to agree to:

- Design in an interdisciplinary manner;
- Avoid gimmicks and oversizing;
- Make the landscape and biodiversity fundamental to the design;
- Carry out community consultation and to keep the community informed;
- The use of only healthy and benign materials;
- Set targets for energy and water consumption;
- Minimise expenditure on building services through passive design;
- Optimise passive use of building form and fabric;
- Be creative in meeting the key issues outlined in the Introduction;
- A sustainable development policy statement;

- **Seek the best possible guidance on sustainability issues to ensure a contemporary and holistic approach;**
- **Consult with stakeholders including future user groups;**
- **Think long-term and adopt life-cycle costing;**
- **Be prepared to innovate with the right advice;**
- **Think through building control and management and consider those that need to be involved;**
- **Develop, early on, a handover strategy with the eventual user;**
- **A feedback strategy (including post-occupancy appraisal) and terms of engagement;**
- **Meet regularly during the defects liability period.**

A formal, thorough appraisal should always be undertaken at the outset of a project if the client or client body is to be sure that the building will meet their requirements and be the right building in the right place.

This might best include:

- Familiarisation with the client or client organisation, the nature of their project and any identified site;

- Identifying any history of the project, which may have a bearing on attitudes, responsibilities and likelihood of success in sustainability terms. This might include the past involvement of members, funders, the affected community or planners, and the current attitudes to the project;

- Clarifying and recording the client's motivation, their goals and objectives in the short and longer terms. In the case of a multiple client/community clients this may require additional resources;

- Establishing the extent of professional services required and satisfying yourself that the scope is sufficient to enable a truly integrated and sustainable approach, or identifying and specifying additional skills required. Some design teams and clients will benefit from specialist handholding services to guide the sustainability agenda;

- Establishing robust lines of communication and identifying procedures to be used in the event of a need for clarification by the client/client body or their representative and the project team;

- Identifying the client's environmental/functional/operational priorities;

- Informing the client(s) of relevant sustainability issues and any benefits resulting from sustainable design, such as community engagement, improved manageability, waste and pollution prevention, cost-in-use benefits, user satisfaction, health benefits, increased productivity and/or reduced environmental liability; highlighting:
  - strategic sustainability issues of generic importance to all projects such as location, form and orientation, attention to detail, infrastructure, manageability, usable controls, appropriate tender procedures, performance targeting and integration;
  - sustainability issues of particular relevance to the client activity or priorities, using these to establish whether there is a real need to build, and using the priorities to set a relevant sustainability policy or vision for the project and an agenda for future discussions with all parties;

- Agreeing with the client that sustainable design brings with it a need to commit to some basic principles and that it may involve challenging the way they have worked in the past and challenging some professions. Clients must not think that they can pick and choose 'sustainable' and 'non-sustainable' aspects.

- Establishing with the client(s) the value of participation in the design process by those who will be involved in the success of the building in the long term, and recommending an approach that encourages user community and/or local community input in achieving social and environmental sustainability:

- identify with the client who should be involved at this stage and seek their involvement or that of appropriate representatives. This should involve the eventual users and affected community (user community and/or local community) as well as building operators and management. It may be necessary to establish with the client(s) the value of participation in the design process by a broader community – those who will be involved in the success of the building in the long term – and to recommend an appropriate professionally managed approach;

- Using brainstorming, workshops or other appropriate techniques for defining the project clearly and comprehensively, including the client's and design team's aspirations, and any project-specific opportunities;

- Making the client(s) aware of capital and revenue implications of decisions. High aspirations may unlock additional funds externally, if there is real drive for innovation or engagement. In general this type of funding will aim to create a level playing field for a better project rather than generating capital funding. Alternatively the client may look to internal funding if genuine functional/marketing or cost-in-use benefits can be quantified;

- Considering a number of different procurement methods. It will be useful to think through the appropriate procurement, design and tender procedures that could affect the sustainability criteria in addition to the conventional client or client body requirements. Include consideration of specific clauses to tie down sustainability aspects and means to really scrutinise claims;

- Advising on implications for cost, timescale and any essential additional services, including any cost in use and marketing benefits.

B: Design Brief

The Design Brief provides an opportunity to test the client's requirements and to establish whether they are functionally, economically, socially and environmentally sustainable. This will involve assessing affordability, the relationship of client activities to potential users, and the relationship between building type, activity and site.

A number of options should be assessed. For a building project to take best advantage of the opportunities for environmental and social enhancement these aspects are best placed on the agenda at the outset. If necessary, specialist consultants should be sought.

This Work Stage should produce a brief for the building that fulfils the client's aims and objectives, including environmental performance.

The Briefing Process

The brief is crucial. In addition to the usual briefing issues, the following may need special consideration:

- Use of an accepted design briefing guide or professional advisor to confirm procedures, schedules and budgets;

- Development controls and planning policies relating to biodiversity, travel and community needs;

- Preparing the brief for the feasibility study such that it forms a clear record of the client's needs, requirements and aspirations (building function, activity types anticipated/ preferred location). At this stage the client may wish to discuss the degree of commitment to the sustainability agenda;

- Identifying principal issues of particular importance or relevance to the project function/operation and the client's activities and priorities;

- Ensuring that life-cycle costing is used to inform decision-making that is resource effective.

A sustainable approach will tend to increase emphasis on:

- The central importance of the site, the site history (including placing the building in the urban/rural structure) and biodiversity;

- Analysis and response to climate, landscape, ecology and infrastructure;

- User and community participation to enable opportunities and objections to be identified early on and dealt with to enhance user and community commitment and sense of ownership, to determine revenue implications and to save time further on;

- Using the form and fabric as the primary means of environmental control;

- Setting appropriate targets for energy efficiency and water economy; as well as performance in areas such as materials selection, daylighting and indoor air quality;

- Design for enhanced pedestrian and cycle access and reduced car use – hence the relationship to public transport infrastructure and amenities;

- Specifying benign materials – in relation to minimising embodied energy and embodied toxicity. (Currently much is

made of embodied energy, the amount of energy required
to get a material or product to a site, but it is worth
noting that the vast majority of materials are chemically
as well as mechanically transformed, and they also have
significant embodied pollution beyond that of carbon. A
truly sustainable approach requires the minimisation of *all*
pollution);

- Maximising passive design and reducing the service component
  so that the mechanical systems serve as supplements to natural
  systems rather than replacements for them;

- Enhancing user satisfaction and productivity and health
  concerns, both internally and in the wider environment;

- Affordability, both in terms of first cost and life-cycle
  costs, taking account of trends in policy aimed at reversing
  unsustainable patterns of consumption;

- Arrangements for building management, including user-
  friendly control systems.

The level of client commitment to environmental objectives will
vary, and it might be useful to seek to establish the extent of their
aspirations by a discussion of light to dark green solutions. The
table on pages 26–27 may inform discussion and form the basis for
establishing the level of ambition in the brief, but it is not a rigid
classification or prescription.

Design Team

As a criterion of shortlisting, architects may well be expected to
indicate commitment to care and enhancement of the existing
structure, and to demonstrate that they understand and respect
cultural and heritage implications. With this in mind, they may wish
to consider joining a Conservation Architect Scheme, such as that run
by the RIAS. Similarly, clients may require evidence of commitment
to sustainable design and so architects may wish to look to the
Sustainable Architects Scheme. Clients may wish to look to current
lists of architects registered under such schemes.

Table 1 Some aspects of Gaia's six principles

Extended tables under these headings have been developed by the author for the Gaia Group to assist clients to set briefs and inform planning applications.

	Below Acceptable Level	Acceptable Level	Higher Level	Highest Level
MANAGE THE PROCESS				
Site Practice	No control	Third-party accreditation, e.g. Considerate Constructors Scheme (CCS) or CEEQUAL	CCS/CEEQUAL agreed target	CCS/CEEQUAL Excellent
Briefing and Audit Policy	No policy	Published policy agreed by principal partners with clear objectives	Comprehensive policy	Comprehensive third-party appraised policy and use of a process guide
Design Quality	No control	Appraisal by approved body and response actioned	Proactive pursuit of design quality	
Post-occupancy Assessment	No policy	Agreement to independent audit of resource consumption after first year	Post-occupancy community and resource audit	Ongoing proactive post-occupancy audit
Building Label	No target	Consideration based on solutions appropriate to the context		
Transport and Access	No policy	Green Travel Plan with public transport and well developed pedestrian/cycle access to local amenities such as schools, shops and leisure facilities		Active pursuit of low impact travel and safe pedestrian routes to amenities
Biodiversity	No target	Adherence to local biodiversity plan to protect existing ecological features	Biodiverse rich areas with wildlife corridor and maintenance strategy	Full biodiverse rich landscape over 50% of area
Resources	No target	Ecofootprint appraisal	Ecofootprint appraisal – to agreed target	'One planet' limit
Health – Materials	No policy	Policy on selection of healthy materials	Exclusion list	Allergy-free specification
Consultation with Community	None	Undertake consultation and record and distribute the outcomes	Establish consultation and self-management group/residents association with an agenda of essential issues	
Designing Out Crime	No policy	Approved details and a policy that provide an unobtrusive approach to the creation of secure, quality places where people wish to live and work		
SUPPORT COMMUNITY				
Food Cultivation	No productive landscape or cultivation provision	Proportion (10%) of edible landscape	A third of bushes and trees yield edible produce	Residents given opportunity to cultivate in allotments or private space
IT/Community Web	No IT infrastructure	IT infrastructure and provision of space, and services, for a home office	Integrated local community web net/ communication tool with local information on environment, transport and food, such as green mapping	
Public Space	No attention to public space, meeting places or amenity	High quality public environment which combines visual attraction and security		Community involvement in design of public space

Special Community Project	None	Designed meeting places	A common facility specified, designed and managed by the community	
ENHANCE BIODIVERSITY				
Plant Selection and Habitat	No policy	Appropriate habitat types	Varied native flora and low water requirement species	Landscape design promoting biodiversity of plant habitats
Timber	Fear of timber	FSC or equivalent third-party label	No tropical timber	Use of local timber
Gardens	No policy	Designed open and private space	Private open space to 50% of properties	All properties with private open space
CREATE HEALTHY ENVIRONMENTS				
Materials and Moisture	Standard solution	Provision of separate indoor drying space	Moisture transfusive construction	Hygroscopic materials used throughout
Noise	Standard solution	Pre-completion testing of compliance	Significant improvement over the regulatory requirements	
Colour	Standard solution	Normal practice	Full-project colour strategy	
Electromagnetic Smog	Standard solution	Normal practice	Non-ring main	
USE RESOURCES EFFECTIVELY				
Primary Energy – Overall	Standard solution	50% of building regs	30% of building regs	20% of building regs
Water Consumption	Not considered	Low water use fittings and dual flush toilets and calculations to show options	Rainwater collection system for landscaped areas	Rainwater collection optimised, based on cost calculation
Cycling	No consideration	Cycle storage for 20% of dwellings and safe secure parking at local amenities	Cycle storage for 50% of dwellings and safe secure parking at local amenities	Cycle storage for all dwellings and safe secure parking at local amenities
Community Waste Plan	None	Provision of internal or external storage	Robust plan for waste and recycling	Local Ecostation for recycling
Solar Design/ Orientation	No consideration	Bioclimatic approach to sun and shelter		Modelled and quantified
Adaptability / Multi-use	Unnecessary constraints	Standard solution	Adaptability in 10% of dwellings	Adaptability in 25% of dwellings
Renewable Contribution	Not considered	Calculations to show what is sensible	Proactive pursuit of sensible affordable, 10% minimum	Proactive pursuit of sensible affordable, 20% minimum
Design for Reuse/ Deconstruction	Standard solution	Some reclaimable items		Approved details
MINIMISE POLLUTION				
Embodied Energy	Not considered	Calculated	Not more than 30 ecopoints/m^2	Not more than 25 ecopoints/m^2
Reduction of Surface Runoff	No surface water, flood or pollution control	Reducing peak runoff rates by 50%	Management and creative use of rainwater for varied ecosystems and landscape	
Halogens	Extensive use of PVC	Avoidance of PVC with exceptions in electric cables and the sewage system		Total avoidance of PVC
Timber Treatment	Standard toxic treatments	No wood preserver except beech distillates or CKB-salts outside the building		No wood preserver throughout

It may be useful to establish criteria for selection of the design team, including:

- Track record, commitment to interdisciplinary working and sustainable design, demonstrated, for example, by membership of the RIAS Accreditation Scheme or similar. The client should seek to discriminate between architects claiming knowledge of the issues and those who have made a genuine contribution to sustainable design, even at a small scale;

- The extent to which a candidate can demonstrate the desire and ability to fulfil the client's aspiration in regard to sustainable design, including previous projects and training undertaken;

- The extent of experience in sustainable design is adequate for the job. Partnering or specialist advisors could be considered.

When considering design team members:

- It may be useful to recognise that the scope of professional services agreed should acknowledge that sometimes additional (and difficult to define) inputs are required to design in an interdisciplinary manner without leaving areas of uncertainty;

- Fee structures should reflect the pursuit of a naturally serviced environment based on project or life-cycle cost, the potential for capital and, if appropriate, running cost savings and the levels of interdisciplinary working required, up to and beyond occupation;

- Innovation – or perceived innovation – will tend to increase resource needs. This should be indicated to the client. It may require specialist skills.

Options that demonstrate an understanding of sustainable design/ specification philosophy include:

- Design quality as an overarching requirement;
- Passive solutions in preference to mechanical solutions;
- Considering the environment in and around buildings as well as buildings themselves;
- Waste minimisation throughout the procurement and subsequent lifetime of the building;
- Resource conservation;
- Enhancing biodiversity through the use of native planting and avoidance of toxins;
- Minimising embodied pollution and toxicity in all its forms with respect to personal and global health;
- A preference for local skills and labour, with acknowledgement of local building traditions and local materials where possible and appropriate, but not as an excuse for pastiche;
- Life-cycle costing in preference to simple capital cost regimes;
- Encouragement of community input to achieve social and environmental sustainability;
- Optimum use of natural light and fresh air to meet user needs, and moisture management to create healthy indoor environments;
- Minimisation of dependence on polluting forms of transport;
- Strategic resource-saving measures to meet specific targets;
- Usability and manageability as crucial long-term design aspects and their role in facilitating this;
- Setting a number of specific quantitative targets for third-party appraisal for the materials, products, buildings and landscape; but also recognising and being attentive to the qualitative aspects;
- Benchmarking and feedback.

This is the best stage to identify appropriate clauses, targets and benchmarks for the different professions to demonstrate commitment and to anchor environmental design.

Seek to persuade the client of the importance of appointing appropriate members of the design team as soon as they can usefully contribute, so that an interdisciplinary approach is emphasised from the earliest opportunity. A team approach will enable a more creative and efficient use of form and fabric and better functionality and manageability than would be achieved by individuals working in isolation.

Site Selection

Where it is an option, consider the relative merits of a number of sites and/or buildings to determine which may best suit the client's requirements. This should be an iterative process, with consideration of options between new build, refurbishment and acquisition and how the client's requirements might be integrated into existing urban, suburban or rural structures. Refurbishment and reuse of existing structures, where achievable, is likely to be preferable to new build. Consideration may take the form of building and/or site appraisals as well as community, culture and financial feasibility.

Before opting for one site and/or building it is useful to consider whether:

- The impact on the local environment has been adequately assessed. This may take the form of a statutory or voluntary environmental impact assessment (EIA). CEEQUAL can also be used positively to address best practice aspirations;

- It may assist the site selection process if an indication of the 'base load' of the project under best practice conditions is established. It might take the form of an estimate of resource throughput (water, energy, power requirements), traffic flows, emissions, noise creation or other implications. Pay particular attention to special processes or needs and to access, public transport, neighbouring buildings, environments or features. Attention to sustainable design is likely to minimise the adverse impacts and the infrastructure and therefore make the project more attractive. However, ensure that the base load is realistic and achievable. Clients should consider making the minimisation of adverse impacts on a community and the environment a contractual obligation.

Drawing on the EIA or similar appraisal, this would be an appropriate time to investigate the potential for fuel saving and damage mitigation of environmental intrusions or waste through a strategic approach to the site such as microclimate assessment, biodiversity appraisals, local transport networks, local topography, lie of water courses, potential for land forming and so on. These are all potentially positive contributions to the design solution.

This would also be the right time to consider how the building is to be used and how this usage may change over time, such as possible extensions, alterations and flexibility of use.

Consultation at this early stage with local, statutory and utility authorities and non-government organisations (such as the Environment Agency and the Scottish Environment Protection Agency) can highlight any problems and provide valuable information for integration into the project, and so prevent abortive work.

C: Concept

Successful Concept Designs involve the presentation of a design concept based on key, focused feasibility studies. By this Work Stage the location of the building, a schedule of accommodation and long-term objectives (including sustainability aspirations) for the building or site will all have been determined.

At this point new design team members may be introduced to the project and their commitment to interdisciplinary design and sustainability should be checked when they are appointed. For example, the six key issues described at the outset (see page 9) could form a basis for discussion of their experience and commitment. Any lack of experience should be identified and appropriate guidance should be sought – possibly as a supplementary service – including training for design team members and specialist advice. This may relate to specific sustainability issues, objectives and targets, or to process aspects such as interdisciplinary working and critical path analysis for sustainable design. It is important to reinforce the need to deliver reliable good practice rather than 'green' technology gimmicks.

The following measures will probably be useful.

- It may be beneficial for the client and design team to briefly review Work Stages A and B in order to confirm that the brief is a proper expression of the client's needs, requirements and aspirations. It should also explicitly incorporate the priorities and any targets that may be necessary to achieving the economic, social and environmental success of the project;

- This is the time to firmly establish the required performance targets, for example using independently published best practice guidelines or key performance indicators (KPIs). These should ensure that standards are set as high as possible in relation to biodiversity, resources, pollution, community engagement and health, and that they fully exploit the experience of the team;

- The team may wish to work together to establish their sustainability aspirations;

- Affected communities (including future building users and managers) should be engaged in discussion on the project, and their views taken seriously. Community consultation is a specialist activity and resources should be allocated to undertake it professionally;

- Passive design strategies and building form and fabric should be emphasised as principal climate moderators;

- However, innovative techniques should be investigated and their benefits in quality and cost terms calculated against more established techniques. We need to innovate;

- Discuss the opportunities related to life-cycle costing with clients and, where possible, look for design assessments and system decisions to be accompanied by life-cycle information. Include factors related to infrastructure, product specification and maintainability of the structure and fabric. Look for a long design life, especially for expensive items;

- Choose and economise on materials as a composite part of initial thinking to ensure an efficient, appropriate and benign structure;

- Undertake a formal audit of materials that could be obtained from local or recycled sources, and inform the client and others of any cost or contractual implications and any local benefits;

- Make the landscaping a composite part of initial thinking;

- As far as possible use the landscape, building orientation, form and structure as the climate moderators. This requires an integrated approach to the development of structure, form and landscape. They should not be either isolated or sequential activities;

- Place the building or buildings to take account of the urban or rural pattern of development and the opportunities offered for integration with transport infrastructure, community integration through work and play, and resource management through consideration of light and shade. Knowledge of the geography and topography can inform microclimate design;

- Identify the functions and demands of each of the spaces, including external or semi-external spaces and their environmental requirements. If appropriate, identify formal zones of the building for control purposes based on how the building is to be used. This makes assessment of demand and control easier;

- Assess potential negative aspects of climate, such as the dilemma between useful solar gain and overheating and glare;

- Consider wastes arising in the different spaces and start to develop a waste strategy;

- Review all passive opportunities for environmental design prior to initial assumptions about mechanical servicing;

- Identify areas with specialist requirements (heating, cooling, ventilation, acoustic and lighting needs may all be relevant) and deal with them separately rather than raising the servicing needs of the building overall;

- All systems should be efficient and controllable to reduce internal gains and waste;

- Be explicit about controls.

Resolving the interconnections between spatial, structural, constructional, indoor climate and services requirements at the end of Work Stage C is particularly important. Mismatches at this Work Stage will add cost later.

Specific Tasks for Consideration at Work Stage C

It is worthwhile for the design team and client to work together to determine priorities based on the key principles highlighted in the introduction. The following provides an outline, but detailed guidance is provided in publications identified in the references section.

Fabric, Form and Orientation

These aspects are crucial. It is important to maintain an energy-efficient form and to optimise the performance of the fabric in relation to climate to minimise servicing requirements. Prevailing wind, solar and rain conditions can be significant determinants of orientation, but be imaginative, not dogmatic, to make the best of passive solar design, neighbourhood issues, massing and views.

Materials

Materials play an important role. The form of a building can influence the choice of materials; equally, appropriate choice of materials can reduce the ventilation needs and aid the relative humidity regime in a building. Promoting the use of local materials (timber, bricks, recycled materials) can contribute to reduced embodied energy and benefit the local economy, but materials must be suitable and affordable. Respecting local character and culture of material use can make a genuine contribution to the locality; it need not be pastiche.

It is important to design for flexibility, repair and deconstruction. Toxic and/or unhealthy materials and treatments should be avoided, especially where they impact on the indoor environment. There are many alternatives to polluting hydrocarbon-based materials, and attention to detail will minimise or eliminate the need for treatments.

Lighting/Daylighting

Building design and orientation should optimise daylight, but avoid unintended solar gain, glare and direct sunlight which can cause discomfort and increase servicing needs. It takes time and modelling to optimise, but this need not be difficult or expensive and it is worth taking that time to enable the best decisions to be made.

Controls

Controls are a vital strategic aspect of design and need to be thought through from the outset in relation to room and equipment layout, and throughout the design process in relation to function and management. Establish zones and related control strategies according to occupancy and use. Incorporate all zones of a building (including any external areas) into a control strategy.

Landscape

Environmentally beneficial opportunities exist in outdoor, semi-climatic and indoor spaces and where these interface. Consider the benefits of using the landscape for shelter and microclimate and as more than amenity value indoors. Indoor plants are increasingly used for climate moderation. Design for external comfort. Ensure that landscape strategies do not depend on high-maintenance techniques with adverse environmental impact, such as chemical treatment. The requirement for water management (Sustainable Urban Drainage Systems) is an example of where perceived environmental constraints have presented creative opportunities in infrastructure saving, pollution prevention and water conservation for amenity and enhancing biodiversity as a landscape element.

Urban Design

Identify planning and design controls that have an environmental relevance, and use the building project as a means to promote and advance local sustainability policies. Support the development and maintenance of healthy mixed-use neighbourhoods and communities. Promote the full involvement of all stakeholders in development issues. Consider shared functions (walls/heating/access management, etc.) between neighbour buildings. Provide safe open-space environments for exercise and socialisation. Maintain a biodiverse habitat. Encourage a superefficient, diverse, integrated transport system.

Energy Requirements and Power Generation

Aim to minimise load requirements strategically, to save on infrastructure or upgrading and costs. However, be wary of chasing efficiencies at the margins at the expense of improved quality overall.

Fire

Avoid PVC-based materials and components. Note that timber is being revisited as an acceptable material under fire regulations. Proactive fire engineering at an early stage can generate innovative passive design possibilities and avoid the need for fire retardants which are an environmental toxin.

Heating

Minimise heating needs by appropriate orientation, form, layout and proper glazing/insulation, but not at the expense of internal inefficiencies in lighting and so on. Eliminate air infiltration in favour of designed ventilation. Then, after minimising demand, aim to use the least polluting sources of energy for heating. Identify any local energy sources (wood, straw, wind, geothermal) but avoid adding unnecessary expense and maintenance costs. Formalise a complete and clear design brief to ensure that the operational needs are understood and can be taken into account at the outset. Consider the use of combined heat and power systems for large loads, where high maintenance is an acceptable overhead and where there is a summer heating load.

Waste

Look to resource effectiveness in designing the structure. For example, consider prefabrication, low impact foundations, use of recycled materials (without embodied toxicity) and design for recycling. Also consider the opportunities and provision for recycling during the building operation.

Noise

Think about the noise regime in a building or scheme. Position plant and routes that may give rise to disturbance away from sensitive areas. Plan to minimise noise pollution from traffic and local sources, particularly if noise may undermine the project or increase servicing requirements (i.e. by preventing the use of natural ventilation). It is worthwhile at this stage giving consideration to how the project will be built and the access needs of constructors, to minimise noise pollution to neighbours, or to other aspects of the project if it is to be phased.

Transportation and Conveying Systems

Avoid the use of mechanical conveying systems such as lifts and escalators, except for essential use and disabled access. Discourage their non-essential use and encourage use of stairs through appropriate layouts. Ensure that any systems do not use asbestos.

Ventilation and Cooling

Make strategic decisions regarding reduction of internal and external gains based on thermal mass, solar shading, night cooling and, where appropriate, openable windows/atria to minimise or eliminate a need for mechanical cooling. Investigate a range of strategies from the outset and be aware of the need to integrate with fire, noise and thermal control considerations. Consider the ventilation requirements of the different spaces independently rather than looking for one overriding strategy. Undertake option appraisals to identify the most appropriate, efficient, manageable and occupant-friendly solution. Reduce summer heat gains through appropriate orientation and fabric design including airtightness. Buildings must be airtight so that, whatever the system, it can operate as efficiently as possible. Seek specialist input on airtightness detailing. Aim to achieve as much as possible passively. Strategically plan for occupants to change their environment to improve conditions, for example provide operable windows.

Renewable Energy

There is no direct need for renewable technology to be included for a building to be considered sustainable. Some technologies are expensive and impractical, being themselves the source of waste and pollution; and renewable energies can put pressure on ecosystems. Passive measures such as airtightness, insulation and low embodied energy should take higher priority. Ecominimalism has much to recommend it (see www.gaiagroup.org/Architects/ecominimalism_ BFF_06.pdf). However, opportunities for renewable energy should be considered in order to identify viable opportunities that are appropriate to the site and the available resources. This should only be done once the basics have been dealt with and not in such a way that money is spent chasing marginal gains at the expense of the bigger picture.

Water Provision and Treatment

Water conservation and wastewater treatment require early strategic decisions. An audit of water supply and demand is essential. Early decisions about collection, usage, conservation and treatment can be significant determinants of the infrastructure and may impact on form and surrounding land requirements. The costs of water and waste in use are very significant and so it is worth allowing sufficient time to design efficient systems. Avoid single-issue solutions. Consider as wide a picture as is practical and appropriate, including function, maintenance, water use, effluent quality, chemical use, energy consumption, materials, land use and aesthetics. Make lists of site-specific issues and opportunities and prioritise them. Pay attention to efficiency measures, as they are almost always cheaper and more environmentally benign than recycling. Reproducibility and public acceptability may be more important than absolute environmental performance, but for very sensitive sites, radical solutions and changes in personal habits will be necessary. Do not compromise health.

Co-ordination

Ensure that the design team and client share the decision-making on strategic issues.

D: Design Development

The Concept Design (Work Stage C) should have clarified the strategic approach and should have set benchmarks for the building's performance. Work Stage D is the time to focus on teamwork and to take the project forward to planning permission with a cost plan, signed off by the client.

The ability of the architect to determine best practice beyond outline proposals will inevitably be limited in some areas by lack of specialist knowledge. Hence the whole of the design team, with the client, needs to agree on targets. Ideally, these could be reinforced by incentives that include enforceable penalties as well as proper rewards.

At this stage it would be advisable to:

- Assert principles and a design philosophy established in Work Stage C and develop issues to be addressed by all design team members, using targets and benchmarks. These should ensure that the standards set are as high as possible and fully exploit the experience of the team. Gaia has been developing briefing mechanisms with a range of clients that incorporate qualitative and quantitative aspects. These include guidelines such as BREEAM (the Building Research Establishment Environmental Assessment Methods), and KPIs that can inform an agenda but resist the tendency for quantitative aspects to limit the aspirations of the design;

- Ensure that environmental issues and targets are on the agendas of all design team and progress meetings;

- Timetable specific design co-ordination meetings to ensure an interdisciplinary approach and to avoid the need for downstream changes;

- Ensure that the community consultation is progressing, and if possible seek suggestions from the local community or affected parties that could benefit the project;

- Keep a watching brief on the materials used in respect of environmental impact;

- Control costs, without compromising environmental principles, or they may well be the first things compromised later.

- Use life-cycle costing to inform decision-making, even at the early stages;

- Give detailed consideration to structure and construction/ buildability, especially when innovating. Ensure that the client is made aware of any departures from what could be construed as conventional;

- Consider a two-stage tender for the building contract based on buildability. Such an approach can mean that buildability issues are discussed early on in the design process and amendments made appropriately, thereby aiding the transition to site and reducing the risk of undermining the environmental approach. If that is possible then use Work Stages F, G and H to select an appropriate contractor;

- Insist on environmentally engineered solutions from building services engineers for ventilation, daylighting, cooling and heating. Validate with an independent environmental advocate if necessary, or link to a fee scale that is related to benchmarks of performance in use (and also independent of equipment supplied). Information on these issues can be at best sketchy and at worst ill-informed. Make sure that team members are familiar with best practice in these matters. The area is a complex one and a degree of learning will be required by all involved;

- Pay particular attention to controls. The **PROBE Studies** are an excellent and concise source of fundamental principles which could form the basis for any dialogue;

- Take account of timescales and availability of products, materials or systems in establishing the lead-in period and be prepared to offer alternatives.

Specific Tasks for Consideration at Work Stage D

Form, Fabric and Orientation

Review the strategy in order to ensure that it is optimised in relation to energy and comfort.

Materials

Vet the specification against a thorough and independent labelling scheme or a list of deleterious materials, considering the overall effect on the ability to source locally, indoor air quality, implications for ventilation strategies and maintainability. Lists have become unfashionable but the consequences are that we have largely failed to address indoor air quality. Check manufacturers' claims. Check maintenance and product reliability, as these are all crucial factors if best practice measures are to perform as expected throughout the design life of the building. If it does what it says on the tin – read the tin!

Lighting/Daylighting

Use the **Lighting and Thermal (LT) Method** or an equivalent to seek to optimise façade performance.

Consider the use of scale models for daylighting assessments – some simple low-cost techniques can provide good information. Calculate the daylight factor for all interior spaces of a building and the lighting throughout the room. Remember, the daylight factor is quantitative.

Ensure that the light quantity **and quality**, fittings and controls will match user and management needs and requirements. Use well-controlled and low-energy lighting and fittings. Ensure that the lighting and daylighting are well integrated and properly controlled. Consider long life and low maintenance issues.

Controls

Use control systems with 'manual and auto off, and manual on'. Separate management and personal controls making the latter visible and clear. Ensure systems are fail-safe and fail-efficient. Seek inbuilt energy and water monitoring with feedback and exception reporting. Insist on diagnostics that simplify fault-finding.

Simplicity is possible – do not be oversold. In the UK there is no need to specify cooling controls at less than 24 degrees Celsius, and higher is acceptable for short periods unless there are special requirements.

Ensure that fans and pumps do not run when not required. This is not a simple request. Avoid excessive humidification.

Landscape

Respect local species, habitats and access, as well as ecological composition, including the impact of previous interventions. Shield entrances of buildings and external areas that could be functional or recreational from prevailing wind and rain. Ensure adequate provision, and access to amenity, for cyclist and pedestrian users. Avoid deleterious materials or the need for polluting chemicals in the landscape strategy: they are a long-term liability.

Urban Design

Make links and interactions with pedestrian and cycle routes, other buildings and spaces as appropriate. Be aware of access and security issues. Design the spaces between buildings for real enjoyment. If you get the opportunity, deal with big issues first of all.

Energy Requirements and Power Generation

Minimise electromagnetic fields – see *The Whole House Book* and the European Biology and Bioelectromagnetics website (www.ebab. eu.com). There is good guidance available on this subject (see the references section).

Reduce energy consumption by specifying efficient systems with good and easily understandable controls. Beware of the tendency to substitute expensive, high-maintenance and short-life renewables where form, fabric and controls would do a better job of reducing energy demand. Undertake an energy assessment using a readily available software package or guide.

Heating

Quantify the heating needs and appropriate controls. Consider using zoning to make best use of buffer zones and to make demand and control easier. Identify fuel sources and possible supply issues. Consider implications of any infrastructural upgrading and alternative strategies offered by form and fabric.

Do not assume the Building Regulations' figures are correct, they may introduce inaccuracies that impact on future comfort and energy. Instead, calculate actual U-value to determine the effects of the structure on the heating plant. Eliminate 'over-engineering'. Specify intrinsically efficient equipment, such as simple heat-reclaiming systems, variable-speed pumps and drives, time and temperature controls with weather compensation and optimum start/stop controls, where applicable. They will be cheaper and much more cost effective than photovoltaic cells. Make use of low-water content plant: less water = less fuel.

Waste

Consider the recycling potential of materials arising on site as a result of client(s) activities. Design for separation of wastes and develop suitable, easy-to-use collection systems for large schemes.

Transportation and Conveying Systems

Only use efficient lifts and escalator systems. Consider location of functions in relation to movement requirements and any benefits from rearranging.

Ventilation and Cooling

Quantify implications of ventilation strategies with properly controlled fan power. On polluted sites, create intermediate climatic zones to precondition incoming air. Quantify the cooling needs and look to benign methods. Beware the tendency for fads. Seek examples, numbers or benchmarked guarantees. Avoiding refrigerant is readily possible, but beware the tendency to introduce inefficiencies, excessive fan power or complications. Ensure that all mechanical plant is efficient, cleanable and properly controlled. Confirm the airtightness details with approved specialists. Do not locate air intakes and opening windows where pollution and noise are at their highest. To reduce ventilation requirements and improve the indoor air quality, specify non-polluting materials, and materials and finishes that do not emit harmful gases (such as formaldehyde or VOCs) into the internal environment (non-off-gassing materials). Extract internally generated pollutants at source.

Combustion appliances should be room-sealed to avoid the requirement for uncontrollable, open-air vents. Ensure that cooling systems make use of outside air for free cooling where possible. Design intrinsically energy-efficiency, low-velocity systems with lower pressure drops.

Water Provision and Treatment

Specify spray taps and low flush WCs. Be aware of the difference between rainwater, black water (sewage waste) and grey water (sink, washing machine waste). The latter can be the most difficult to deal with – grey water recycling is a specialist activity, because the contents are diverse and often unknown, and often will not be justified by the management requirements.

Consider rainwater collection, in the context of cost and availability of water supply, for toilet flushing and other non-potable uses, but avoid standing water because it can be a hazard. Cleansing systems such as reed beds for black and grey water can add landscape amenity but may not always be justified. When preparing SUDS schemes, aim as far as possible for a pipe-free design. Consider the risks imposed by the construction phase and plan sacrificial areas if necessary. Use low-cost submetering because it allows performance to be measured and problems to be sorted. Do not underestimate the importance of detail and quality in design and installation.

Co-ordination

Where issues are unresolved, avoid increasing the services. For instance, if temperatures may occasionally rise above comfort levels with a passive system but will be cost-, maintenance- and energy-intensive to resolve, then discuss the implications with the client to determine an efficient, and not oversized, solution. Ensure the building's users are aware of how the system is expected to work and how the systems should be managed and maintained. Define operations and maintenance strategies. Review co-ordination of spatial, structural, constructional, indoor climate and services requirements.

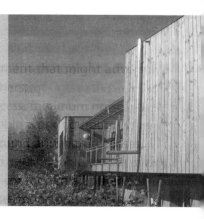

E: Technical Design

The scheme design should have been signed off by the client as a strategically binding agreement.

Work Stage E is the opportunity for consolidation to address all statutory requirements and to seek to meet and even exceed relevant targets. This would be a good time to revisit the original brief and the sustainable design policy, intentions and commitments. New team members may be appointed or there may be changes in responsibility. It is important to ensure that everyone involved understands the issues to date and is adequately trained to implement the requirements.

This is the point at which integration of structure, services, materials and site is essential, and robust means of consolidation and review are required between members of the design team. The team also needs to plan ahead for specification and buildability if environmental targets are to be achieved. Forward thinking about key elements for inclusion in tender documentation is required.

At this Work Stage, the following points should be considered:

- It will assist in the development of the project if a strategic approach is taken to assessment of environmental credentials of suppliers and contractors, including a pre-qualification statement for materials and products. This may exclude specific materials and nominate others;

- Appraise the availability of local materials and confirm whether they are available and are suitable in terms of the key principles;

- Identify where there may be lead times for environmental materials, products or systems and ensure that these are highlighted when going forward to tender documentation;

- Ensure that the affected community is aware of the project progress and timescales and recognises that their input is a valued part of the process;

- Identify specific aspects of the construction where performance to a defined standard will require post-construction testing and validation, including airtightness. Ensure that these are highlighted as a matter for tender documentation;

- Revisit the guidance given in Work Stage C as a special agenda item, to ensure that there are no conflicts arising between the different requirements, and that only the most efficient and resource-conserving systems (conveying systems, heating, cooling, water, lighting) have been specified (and without oversizing);

- Revisit the guidance in Work Stage C with regard to materials, indoor environment, communities and biodiversity;

- Even at this stage, ensure that handover and commissioning of systems have been considered;

- Revisit the issue of building management and user control for efficiency and comfort to ensure that the person(s) responsible for managing the completed building are fully in agreement with the requirements and the strategy;

- Insist on assessments of predicted energy consumption in use as a basis of selection between systems. Check that targets can still be achieved. If appropriate, develop these into life-cycle cost studies for presentation to the client to inform decision-making;

- Involve client/users/operators in discussions on issues concerning maintenance and operation in order to ensure that procedures are fully planned, are affordable and adequate, with minimum adverse environmental impact;

- Create a list/schedule of reductions to be used in the event of the project cost being over budget. Do not target the sustainability aspects. They should at this stage be so fully integrated with the perception of project quality in the minds of design team and client that compromising them would be impossible;

- Identify aspects where cost reductions would seriously undermine environmental objectives;

- Ensure that the agreed targets can and will be achieved and sign off the building design to avoid abortive work. If you are using third-party appraisal schemes this involves paperwork; make sure that there is a budget and if possible tie it to a life-cycle budget and quality agenda.

F/G: Production Information and Tender Documentation

The Production Information should include all the information relevant to the performance of the construction process in relation to the completed building. The responsibilities of each of the parties should be explicit, and agreed targets should have been validated by this Work Stage, along with the control measures that will ensure their operation. The proposed process to be followed in delivering the completed building should be finalised.

Documentation and interviews that relate to the creation of shortlists for tenderers should explicitly refer to site environmental policy and practice, and commit contractors to complying with the requirements of the Considerate Constructors Scheme, or similar. Seek to inform contractors of the additional benefits to them of good practice. It may be that incentives can be identified, such as reduced landfill disposal costs from recycling, increased efficiency from better site management, improved community relations and improved health from lack of on-site treatments.

Consider the following:

- It is advisable to prepare the Tender Documentation in such a way that the bidding contractors recognise the importance of good normal practice with regard to environmental issues;

- An environmental policy statement for the work and explicit contract documentation with targets (and even incentives based on a decommissioning plan) should ensure that contractors make allowance, including time, for environmental matters, procurement and planning of environmental matters or specialist consultation;

- Establish a communication system between bidding contractors and relevant public and private authorities that can advise and assist them on matters such as water management, recycling and local materials;

- Consider a training session for potential bidding contractors to discuss innovative aspects of the design that may add cost due to the 'fear factor';

- Establish systems for checking the environmental commitment of contractors and on-site validation procedures;

- This is the opportunity to set performance targets for issues arising from the construction process, such as noise creation, emissions, discharges and landfill, and to integrate these into the contractors' method statements. This may also include a requirement for contractors to take responsibility for achieving set targets under the CEEQUAL and/or BREEAM schemes;

- The design team should have established performance targets for the completed building. Each member of the design team could take the opportunity to identify these, and highlight any potentially undermining factors and appropriate mitigation strategies;

- Highlight key environmental elements in the Tender Documentation, especially allowing for specific environmental aspects in the chosen system for co-ordination of information;

- Where specific materials are nominated or excluded make this explicit and indicate where any lead times are likely to be an issue;

- Establish a strategy with the building's operator – who may be the client, a client representative, the future tenant, the building management contractor, or other – to embrace all the relevant issues. Put this on the agenda for site meetings at appropriate intervals. It is vitally important that there is a dialogue with the future users, either directly or through a committed third party;

- Be clear that issues impacting on environmental performance can be managed through to handover and operation. Verify that the controls and operational aspects that are intended to assist in meeting targets are not prey to cost-cutting;

- Ensuring that the successful contractor takes responsibility for building maintenance issues during the construction and defect liability periods will probably aid a smooth handover;

- The project will probably benefit if the pre-start site meeting reinforces the environmental issues, including health and safety benefits;

- Commit the design team and contractor to returning as much of the site to its natural state or to enhancing the site with sound landscape practice informed by ecological design;

- Commit the contractor to ensuring that authorities and neighbours are kept up to date at relevant stages in the project development.

H: Tender Action

If the contractor and the site architect or project manager have conflicting priorities then tensions may arise or the sustainability strategy may be undermined. For this reason the tendering process is vital in establishing the appropriate climate in which the work will be undertaken and specific objectives will be achieved.

Construction to handover then becomes a process of reinforcing the agreed objectives. If appropriate procedures are put in place then the tendering process should provide clarity and produce viable tenders from all parties, with sustainability aspects fully addressed. The process of evaluation can then proceed with all bidders being on an equal footing in regard to quality and cost.

It will be highly beneficial to make environmental credentials and experience an issue when preparing a shortlist of potential tenders.

Bidding contractors should be required to join the Considerate Constructors Scheme, or a similar third-party auditable approach to site practice, if they are not already members.

The following points should be considered:

- At pre-tender, the contractors should be asked to provide evidence of their commitment to sustainability, their experience, their understanding of any potential benefits and how these relate to any unique aspects of a project. This information should:

- include a company policy and the method of implementation, including an environmental management system if they have one;
- be specific to the project under tender evaluation and include provision for training of permanent and sub-contract staff;

- As part of the general environmental procedures it will be valuable, and save time in the long run, if a system is established for checking the environmental commitments of sub-contractors and establishing on-site audit procedures;

- Some procurement paths allow for, and encourage, contractor inputs to the planned building process. These should be overseen by the person with direct responsibility for sustainability in order to ensure that there are no adverse implications, in particular changes to the methods of construction, materials and products specification;

- Where performance targets are to be achieved (for example, for airtightness, thermal integrity, monitoring procedures, alarm/fault detection systems), making these an explicit contractual obligation should ensure adequate resources are allowed by prospective contractors, but check that both time and money have been allocated to prevent disputes downstream;

- The contractor should be able to provide evidence that these performance targets can be validated and include method statements and costs of testing and commissioning (including environmentally benign methods of remedying any failings);

- The contractor should be able to provide method statements, targets and information on process issues: waste and resource management, water run-off, and so on;

- Where there are specific environmental considerations to be made in selection of materials and products the contractor should be able to provide evidence that these are understood;

- Identify a member of the design team who can be responsible for advising on environmental aspects of material selection and use, in order to answer questions and appraise changes;

- Put in place procedures for assessing that any schedule of reductions does not undermine the environmental strategy;

- Provide a point of reference to which the contractor may address requirements for validation of changes that may have an environmental implication;

- Identify reporting procedures for failures or outstanding enquiries during routine snagging that have an impact on the sustainability agenda. Allocate clear roles and responsibilities on both sides.

J: Mobilisation

The contractor will have demonstrated clear support for a sustainable approach to the project and Work Stage J is the point at which to fortify this. Many of the points listed below should have been addressed during earlier Work Stages, but now is the opportunity to ensure that the objectives are maintained throughout the construction process.

Method statements for waste and resource management, water run-off, and so on should be validated and agreed, along with procedures for checking sustainability matters and targets with the main contractor.

Method statements, targets and information for all sub-contractors on sustainability matters and procedures should be made available.

The construction process will probably benefit from the following considerations:

- A plan should be drawn up with the successful contractor which takes account of environmental matters, costs, benefits and potential hazards. This should explicitly encourage:

    - orderliness;
    - protection of existing ecology, in so far as it is not directly affected by the works;

- avoidance of any on-site treatment that might adversely affect health of workers or others;
- good neighbourliness (safe access, minimum noise, vibration, litter and dust, sociable working hours, minimum discharges to air, ground and watercourses, access to information);
- maintenance of materials and components in their highest value state to maximise opportunities for resale, reuse and recycling;
- separation of recyclable elements;
- safe disposal of remaining materials;

- Where the project involves some demolition work, reference should be made to Work Stage N in this guide;

- A successful contractor not operating the Considerate Constructors Scheme, or similar third-party approved scheme, should be required to do so, or at the very least should be required to integrate the following into training and managerial procedures in a way that provides transparent and auditable information:

  - preventing run-off;
  - reducing waste by sorting and other means;
  - safety procedures – notably in using materials where risks may have been identified but not proven;
  - ordering of specifically environmental materials with long lead times;
  - selecting products, materials and processes;
  - creating an appropriate line of enquiry on environmental matters, which runs for the duration of the site works;
  - implementing the method statements and keeping the necessary records (the contractor's representative should be responsible for regulating site practice);

- A means of communicating the policy to employees and sub-contractors should have been identified;

- There should be mechanisms in place for briefing sub-contractors on environmental issues and procedures;

- Environmental and community issues must be firmly on the agenda for site meetings – **and not as the last item**;

- A pre-start environmental audit of the site should be used to establish the existing state and act as a record for future practice;

- If there is no plan in place then the design team and contractor should be encouraged to return as much of the site to its natural state as possible, or to enhance the site with sound landscape practice informed by ecological design;

- Authorities and neighbours should be kept up to date following reviews and at any relevant stages in the project development;

- The need for attention to detail where post-completion testing has been specified should be continually reinforced to ensure that it is properly understood and not left to become a remediation issue.

K: Construction to Practical Completion

By this Work Stage the successful contractor should have been helped to understand the priorities and reporting procedures relevant to sustainable design. They should have demonstrated that they recognise the benefits to all involved of good site practice reinforced by an environmental policy and a site method statement. The successful contractor will probably have good experience of the benefits and may well have identified commercial, financial, legislative and health and safety benefits in their bid. Nonetheless, it will be necessary to be vigilant and proactive if aims and objectives are not to be diluted.

The following will probably be useful:

- Identify an individual responsible for monitoring the environmental performance of the contractors. The Clerk of Works may be well suited to the task if appropriately briefed. The use of explicit guidance and benchmarks, such as those laid out in the Considerate Constructors Scheme (or similar), will assist and can form the basis for the documentation;

- Where procedures have not been put in place by the contractor to ensure that the environmental objectives of the construction plan are being monitored, it would be worthwhile arranging for the checklist items identified in

Work Stage J to be considered for integration with site procedures;

- Proper handover documentation has the potential to make a significant contribution to the minimising of environmental impact of a building. Take seriously the requirement to prepare a handover report and keep it up to date throughout the works. It is likely to be the most important aspect in ensuring the long-term sustainability of the project. It should include details of all relevant environmental issues specifically related to building materials and building operation, and it should go beyond the minimal requirements in order to ensure that the motivation behind decision-making is understood. Put documentation of handover information on the agenda of site progress meetings;

- Seek to reinforce the processes established for cataloguing changes and, in particular, for assessing the environmental impact of material and system substitutions and amendments which may take place. Periodically check that they are fully used and integrated into the construction processes;

- To ensure the building is optimised, plan to allow adequate resources of time and money for commissioning, and remember that commissioning may need to be undertaken several times during the first year;

- Try to ensure that account is taken of any possibilities of variations in the occupation and use which might have an impact on the commissioning;

- Verify that all involved are aware of and use good practice guidance on commissioning and handover (such as guidance provided by CIBSE and BSRIA) only generally so that all commissioning and testing is completed satisfactorily without purging and dumping of environmentally harmful emissions to air, ground or watercourses;

- The design team would be well-advised to:

- ensure that the client is properly advised on the need for operative training in respect of potential environmental matters and that procedures have been established for the short and long terms;
- encourage and help the building's users and management to understand the systems and controls, and to define (prior to handover) the staff who will be needed to run and maintain the systems;
- ensure that information on the building and building systems is available in the appropriate and secure format (user manuals and operation and maintenance (O&M) manuals) in handover documentation and readily accessible to the appropriate people, which includes: environmental aspects, such as preferred or prohibited materials for cleaning and maintenance; anticipated resource (energy and water) consumption and alarm states; procedures for validating resource consumption, so as to maintain an ongoing performance monitoring report; procedures for post-occupancy evaluation;

- Establish good lines of communication in preparation for the defects liability period.

L: Post Practical Completion

Clients typically expect buildings to work optimally from day one. But, however reasonable the expectation, and however carefully designed the process, they rarely will. Some form of tuning and some form of induction process will generally be necessary. This should be seen by all involved as a crucial part of the design process and not as an add-on extra or as a symptom of failure.

Commissioning will be ongoing to ensure optimised seasonal performance and this should be integrated to ensure that occupants and building managers are well briefed on any operating regimes.

Ideally, there should be a process in place to assist in the smooth transition to an optimally functioning building. This should have been planned for throughout the project and responsibilities should have been assigned.

The period after Practical Completion is the time at which the value of using a formal process to address sustainability will be most appreciated – or the lack of it regretted. It is the time to put in place appropriate feedback mechanisms, the form of which should ideally have been agreed at the outset of the project, to avoid recriminations and backtracking.

Feedback can take many forms and involves widely varying levels of involvement and commitment on the part of the design team. It is generally under-resourced, rarely forming part of any paid agreement for reasons mentioned above. It is also fraught with practical problems of unresolved responsibility and potential liability, particularly in the early stages of a building's operation. Making it a constructive, useful and fair process is a challenge. However, partnering and goodwill from all sides is more likely to deliver an optimally functioning building in the short term than adversarial relationships. More pragmatically, a constructive approach is most likely to deliver repeat work.

The following considerations are relevant:

- The client and the design team should be clear about the purpose of feedback and clarify their responsibilities and liabilities accordingly at an early stage;

- All design team members should demonstrate a commitment to constructive feedback and, if appropriate, this should be spelled out in their contractual responsibilities;

- A final feedback session may take the form of either information gathering and debriefing, or a formal working relationship with the client or full studies, or some combination of these. They should be inclusive of all who have influenced the project as a positive input to future work.

Types of feedback

At one level there is the internal practice of information gathering and debriefing by a design practice. This process is appropriate to the development of professional practice and perhaps information sharing on design and process matters that may inform future work Debriefing may extend to several or all members of the design team, or it may be a specific task carried out by the project manager, and it will feed into the planning process to benefit other projects and environments. A programme of issues to be addressed – or SWOT analysis (strengths, weaknesses, opportunities and threats) – might be the best framework to identify environmental achievements and missed opportunities. In particular, the process by which any sustainability aspirations have been achieved or missed, as the project progressed, is worth attention to benefit future projects.

A temporary or ongoing working relationship with the building's operating staff will provide an opportunity to ensure that they are adequately provided with information on the building's systems and their functions, and that the operating staff have processes in place to identify and remedy faults. This is intended to encourage optimally efficient use of systems, minimisation of resource wastage, effective environmental performance and occupant satisfaction. It may involve ongoing provision of advice, to be entered into O&M manuals, on the building operation, cleaning regimes, controls and management issues. Such a dialogue may also provide useful information for a design team to determine how successful they were overall.

Full feedback studies, such as the **Probe Studies**, have been used to highlight specific issues of relevance to a building, but they will also raise issues of generic interest to the construction procurement cycle. Such studies have highlighted the real performance of buildings in use and have demonstrated the value of feedback to continual improvement in practice and in optimising building operation. These are among the best possible sources of guidance on building performance.

M: Refurbishment

Although not part of the RIBA Outline Plan of Work, refurbishment is included in this guide as a separate Work Stage because it is an important part of the 'cradle-to-cradle' approach of sustainable design.

Caring for material objects is ecologically sound. Refurbishment provides an opportunity to slow depletion of resources and to enhance environmental performance through upgrading of fabric, structure, systems and components, and attending to local ecology and landscape. A conservative or innovative solution will depend on the nature of the project and the required balance between the values of heritage conservation and the opportunities for design intervention.

Refurbishment has particular challenges and constraints, but it represents an enormous creative opportunity.

Old buildings often hold surprises that represent hazards to health, and this very much reinforces the need to utilise benign materials and processes in new construction. Also, in general, buildings being demolished now were constructed in such a way that their demolition generates high quantities of waste, unless particular care is taken. Recently, the introduction of tax and legal penalties for waste disposal activities has encouraged commercial and design interest in refurbishment and recycling. Also, increasing awareness

of the value of physical resources, products and materials, means that design and construction methods are developing to facilitate flexibility and longer life – including design for conversion to new uses and design for deconstruction.

At refurbishment, consider the following:

- As a criterion of shortlisting, architects may well be expected to indicate their commitment to care and enhancement of the existing structure, and to understanding and respecting cultural and heritage implications. For example, they may do this by being members of the various conservation architect schemes. Clients may wish to look to current lists of architects registered under such schemes;

- Bidding contractors should be encouraged to join the Considerate Constructors Scheme, or a similar third-party auditable approach to site practice, if they are not already members;

- When repairing or updating, it is advantageous if the client or client's representative provides an asset register of buildings, contents and components as a starting point for future works and identification of environmental opportunities;

- Different parts of a building – fittings, services, fabric and structure – have different timescales for refurbishment. It would be advisable to undertake an audit of:
  - the existing site and buildings;
  - the existing plant, fabric and structure, based, if possible, on cost-in-use (maintenance and operating costs);
  - environmental impact (pollutants generated and environmental performance);

- Pay attention to structural flexibility of the existing shell;

- Identify any hazardous materials;

- Together with the owners, client group or others, it would be advisable early on to:

  - determine criteria on which buildings, fabric, systems and components are to be upgraded or replaced. This might require consideration of the urban form and consultation on neighbourhood/community needs;
  - use these criteria to identify the optimum combination of removal, alteration and reuse to exploit the site and building elements fully;
  - keep neighbours and authorities informed and updated (where necessary) of plans, timescales and other relevant issues;

- If demolition works are required then consult Work Stage N in this guide at the earliest opportunity to identify opportunities for reuse and recycling;

- Identify the potential reuse and recycling of structures, elements, materials and systems on the site;

- The guidance described above in Work Stages A–L provides good practice guidelines in relation to environmental policy, contractors, tenders and preparations for occupation;

- In design terms, as with new build, aim to move from active to passive solutions (such as optimum use of sunshine, natural light and air) and avoid increasing the servicing requirement. Use mechanical systems as supports for natural systems, not as substitutes for them;

- Where installed systems are to be replaced, aim as far as possible to use high-efficiency components (fixtures and fittings) and good control systems;

- Where systems are judged to be fit for ongoing use, consider the installation of additional controls for lighting, water and heating/cooling. Much can be achieved by consideration of different zones and the use of thermostats, time switches, and so on;

- In refurbishment it is necessary to allow sufficient time and therefore fees for all Work Stages from redesign through to recommissioning. It may be that some elements may involve a balance between time and cost, especially if there are opportunities for income generation or for avoidance of cost. Pay particular attention to:

  - pre-qualification of suppliers and contractors;
  - quality of stripping out and preservation of fabric and components;
  - surprises that the building may hold (structurally or with respect to contaminants) and the contractor's possible response;
  - complexity of services installation and access inside an existing shell;
  - specialist skills at all stages;

- Prepare a handover report and keep it up to date throughout the works.

N: Demolition

Although not part of the RIBA Outline Plan of Work, demolition is included in this guide as a separate Work Stage because it is an important part of the 'cradle-to-cradle' approach of sustainable design.

A presumption in favour of retention and refurbishment of existing buildings should be the norm and there are excellent examples of reuse, change of use and extension to add value to otherwise redundant buildings.

However, regeneration may not always be the appropriate route. Poorly designed buildings can inflict unnecessarily high demands on occupiers by way of poor quality living and working conditions, and can burden owners and operators with excessive running and maintenance costs.

Before opting for demolition, thoroughly investigate the opportunities in relation to new build versus refurbishment (see Work Stage M). This may well be an iterative process in respect of long-term plans for the locality and its culture, the building/site and environmental implications of refurbishment and total or partial demolition.

Where demolition is deemed appropriate then, if undertaken with sensitivity and environmental responsibility, it can be a positive contribution to a community, a location and the wider environment.

The demolition process incorporates three specific phases: decommissioning (to bring a building or site to an inert state – perhaps temporarily); dismantling; and disposal.

- Prepare a decommissioning plan that takes account of environmental matters, costs, benefits and potential hazards. This should explicitly encourage:
    - protection of local ecology;
    - good neighbourliness (adequate information to local communities, safe access, non-obtrusive lighting and security, minimum noise, vibration, litter and dust, sociable working hours, minimum discharges to drains, ground and watercourses);
    - maximum recycling, and therefore maintenance of materials and components in their highest value state to maximise opportunities for resale, reuse and recycling;
    - safe disposal of remaining materials;

- Legal responsibilities and costs in respect of waste disposal and contaminated land have become significantly more onerous in recent years and therefore it is vital to be aware of them;

- Recycling and reuse opportunities have increased alongside penalties for dumping;

- Prior to letting a demolition contract, it will be beneficial to undertake an audit of materials that could be recycled into the supply chain. Publish the list through the appropriate bodies (see the references section) and allow adequate time for responses;

- Information under Work Stages H, J, K and L will assist in the appointment of the appropriate contractor using fully auditable benchmarks, such as the Considerate Constructors Scheme or similar, and appropriately careful tender strategies;

- Prepare the Tender Documentation in such a way that the bidding contractors will recognise the importance of environmental issues. Refer to Work Stages F/G, H and J in this guide. Pay particular attention to the need for:

- an environmental policy statement for the work and explicit contract documentation based on a decommissioning plan – with targets and even incentives – which should ensure that contractors make allowance, including time, for environmental matters;
- method statements for particularly environmentally hazardous aspects of the demolition. These should be validated at tender evaluation;
- attention to those affected in the community with respect to site operations;
- a communication system between bidding contractors and relevant public and private authorities who can advise and assist recycling schemes;
- a system for checking the environmental commitments of contractors and on-site validation procedures;

• Ensure that the building is decommissioned (to an inert state) before demolition begins;

• Prepare a handover report from the outset to cover all matters and keep it up to date throughout the works.

References and Sources of Information

Design

- Papanek, V. (1971) *Design for the Real World: human ecology and social change*, Granada.
- Borer, P. and Harris, C. (1998) *The Whole House Book,* Centre for Alternative Technology Publications.
- Gaia Group (2006) *Design and Construction of Sustainable Schools*, volumes 1 and 2, Scottish Executive (www.gaiagroup.org).
- Liddell, H.L. (2006) *Eco-minimalism*, Green Building Bible Vol. 1, Green Building Press, pp. 98–103 (and www.gaiagroup.org).
- Architecture for Humanity (ed.) (2006) *Design Like You Give a Damn*, Thames & Hudson.
- Halliday, S.P. (2007) *Sustainable Construction,* Butterworth-Heinemann.

History

- Carson, R. (1962) *Silent Spring*, Haughton Mifflin.
- Ward, B. and Dubois, R. (1972) *Only One Earth*, Norton.
- Myers, M. (ed.) (1985) *The Gaia Atlas of Planet Management*, Pan Books.
- World Commission On Environment and Development (WCED) (1987) *Our Common Future*, Oxford University Press.
- Kemp, D.D. (1990) *Global Environmental Issues: a climatological approach*, Routledge.
- Meadows, D., Meadows, D. and Randers, J. (1992) *Beyond the Limits*, Earthscan.
- Grubb, M. *et al.* (1993) *The Earth Summit Agreements: a guide and assessment,* Royal Institute of International Affairs (RIIA)(Chatham House).

- Brenton, T. (1994) *The Greening of Machiavelli*, Earthscan/RIIA.
  Best title award and a really good summary of the way international
  agreements have evolved.
- Middleton, N. and O'Keefe, P. (2003) *Rio plus Ten: politics, poverty and
  the environment*, Pluto Press.

Policy and legislation

- DETR (2000) *Building a Better Quality of Life: a strategy for more
  sustainable construction in the UK*, The Stationery Office (www.
  construction.detr.gov.uk).
- Halliday, S.P. and Stevenson, F. (2004) *Sustainable Construction and the
  Regulatory Framework*, Gaia Research.
- *Securing the Future: The UK Strategy for Sustainable Development*
  (2005), Cm 6467, HMSO (www.sustainable-development.gov.uk/
  publications/uk-strategy/index.htm).
- DEFRA (2006) *Procuring the Future: Sustainable Procurement National
  Action Plan,* DEFRA (www.sustainable-development.gov.uk/publications/
  procurement-action-plan/index.htm).

Economics

- Mishan, E.J. (1967) *The Costs of Economic Growth*, Pelican.
- Schumacher, E.F. (1973) *Small is Beautiful: a study of economics as if
  people mattered*, Blond Briggs.
- Kennedy, M. (1988) *Interest and Inflation-free Money: how to create an
  exchange mechanism that works for everybody*, Permakultur.
- Pearce, D. and Barde, J.-P. (eds)(1991) *Valuing the Environment*, Earthscan.
- Douthwaite, R. (1992) *The Growth Illusion: how economic growth has
  enriched the few, impoverished the many and endangered the planet*,
  Green Books.
- von Weizsacker, E., Lovins, A.B. and Lovins, L.H. (1995) *Factor Four:
  doubling wealth, halving resource use*, Earthscan.
- Hawken, P., Lovins, A.B. and Lovins, L.H. (1999) *Natural Capitalism*,
  Earthscan.
- Kats, G. (2003) *The Costs and Financial Benefits of Green Buildings*,
  California's Sustainable Building Task Force.

Construction Process and Methods

- Brand, S. (1994) *How Buildings Learn*, Viking Penguin.

- Halliday, S.P. (1994) *Environmental Code of Practice for Buildings and their Services*, BSRIA.
- Egan, J. (1998) *Rethinking Construction*, HMSO.
- CIRIA (2000) *Environmental Handbook for Building and Civil Engineering Projects: construction phase*, CIRIA.
- Federal Facilities Council (2002) *Learning From our Buildings: a state-of-the-practice summary of post-occupancy evaluation.* Technical Report 145. National Academy Press.
- Bordass, W. (2003) Learning more from our buildings – or just forgetting less? *Building Research and Information*, vol. 31, no. 5, pp. 406–411.
- Halliday, S.P. (2007) *Sustainable Construction,* Butterworth-Heinemann.
- National Green Specification: www.greenspec.co.uk
- Scottish Ecological Design Association, for three publications: *Design and Detailing for Deconstruction, Design and Detailing for Air-tightness* and *Design and Detailing for Toxic Chemical Reduction* (www.seda2. org/guides/index.htm).

Appraisal Tools and Techniques

- Halliday, S.P. (2007) *Sustainable Construction,* Butterworth-Heinemann, includes a chapter on appraisal tools and techniques, with case studies.
- BREEAM, the Building Research Establishment Environmental Assessment Methods: www.bre.co.uk
- CEEQUAL, the Civil Engineering Environmental Quality Assessment and Award Scheme: www.ceequal.co.uk
- Considerate Constructors Scheme: www.ccscheme.org.uk
- Constructing Excellence, Construction Industry Key Performance Indicators website: www.constructingexcellence.org.uk (choose 'Benchmarking and KPIs').
- Communities and Local Government (2006) *Code for Sustainable Homes,* CLG: www.planningportal.gov.uk/uploads/code_for_sust_homes.pdf
- EcoHomes: www.breeam.co.uk/ecohomes
- Ecological footprints: www.myfootprint.org; www.redefiningprogress. org; www.ecouncil.ac.cr
- Forest Stewardship Council (FSC): www.fsc.org
- GreenPro: www.newbuilder.co.uk
- Probe Studies – downloadable POEs in the public domain, PROBE strategic papers and BUS questionnaires may be obtained by license: www.usablebuildings.co.uk
- RIAS Sustainable Design Accreditation Scheme: www.rias.org.uk
- Sustainable Neighbourhood Audit Process: www.gaiagroup.org
- UK Woodland Assurance Standard (UKWAS): www.ukwas.org.uk

Biodiversity, Ecology and Landscape

- Crowhurst, D. and Woodall, R. (2003) *Biodiversity Indicators for Construction Projects*, CIRIA W005, CIRIA.
- Newton, J., Williams, C., Nicholson, B., Venables, R. *et al.* (2004) *Working with Wildlife: resource and training pack for the construction industry*, CIRIA C587, CIRIA, contains a 20-page table of wildlife law affecting construction projects.
- Benson, J.F. and Roe, M.H. (eds)(2007) *Landscape and Sustainability*, 2nd edition, Taylor & Francis.

Materials Specification

- Berge, B. (1999) *Ecology of Building Materials*, Architectural Press.
- Anderson, J., Shiers, D.E. and Sinclair, M. (2002) *The Green Guide to Specification*, 3rd edition, BRE.
- Royal Commission on Environmental Pollution (2003) *Chemicals in Products: safeguarding the environment and human health*, RCEP.
- Hall, K. (2006) *Green Building Bible*, 3rd edition, Green Building Press (www.greenbuildingbible.co.uk).
- Halliday, S.P. (2007) *Sustainable Construction*, Butterworth-Heinemann, includes chapters on materials and on low-impact construction, with case studies.
- Centre for Alternative Technology (CAT) publishes various information sheets on materials and systems: www.cat.org.uk
- Construction Resources publishes a number of Guidance Notes: www.constructionresources.com
- Greenpeace, *PVC Alternatives Database*: http://archive.greenpeace.org/toxics/pvcdatabase/
- GreenPro – a subscription-based service: www.newbuilder.co.uk
- Salvo publishes e-mail news of materials and services for recycling at www.salvo.co.uk and a materials information exchange at www.salvoMIE.com
- Waste and Resources Action Programme (WRAP): www.wrap.org.uk

Healthy Buildings

- Smith, C.W. and Best, S. (1989) *Electromagnetic Man*, Dent.
- Holdworth, W. and Sealey, A. (1992) *Healthy Buildings*, Longman.
- Nicol, F. and Rudge, J. (2000) *Affordable Warmth for Healthier Homes*, E&FN. Spon.
- Saunders T. (2002) *Boiled Frog Syndrome: your health and the built environm,ent*, Academy Press.

- Halliday, S.P., Chapman, B. and Liddell, H.L. (2005) *Low Allergy Housing*, Gaia Research.
- Liddell, H.L. Gilbert, J. and Haliiday, S.P., *Designing for Chemical Reduction*, Scottish Executive, in preparation: www.seda2.org
- European Biology and Bioelectromagnetics: www.ebab.eu.com
- Healthy Buildings Network: www.healthybuilding.net

Water Systems

- CIRIA C539 (2001) *Rainwater and Greywater Use in Buildings: best practice guidance*, CIRIA.
- Dreiseitl, H., Grau, D. and Ludwig, K.H.C. (2005) *New Waterscapes: planning, building and designing with water*, Birkhauser.
- Grant, N., Moodie, M. and Weedon, C. (2005) *Sewage Solutions: answering the call of nature*, 3rd edition, Centre for Alternative Technology. Introduction to sewage treatment, conventional and alternative.
- Guidance on water management, pollution and SUDs is available from: Scottish Environmental Protection Agency (www.sepa.org.uk) and Environment Agency (www.environment-agency.gov.uk).

Heating, Lighting and Daylighting, Ventilation and Cooling, and Renewable Technologies

There are thousands of publications covering aspects of heating, lighting, daylighting, ventilation and cooling and an extensive range of guidance on renewable technologies going back over three decades. The government-funded Energy Efficiency Best Practice programme and the Action Energy Programme have published guidance on energy usage in buildings for more than 20 years. These documents – case studies (GPCS), good practice guides (GPG), benchmarking guides (ECG) and general information reports (GIR) – are now published by the Carbon Trust and most can be downloaded free of charge.

Some of the early material on specific renewable technologies remains very relevant to the non-specialist. The technical press has contemporary project literature that is often ahead of information contained in books.

The following sources include a few books that you might not find through conventional routes:

- Bell, J. and Burt, W. (1995) *Designing Buildings for Daylight*, BRE.
- BSRIA (1996) *Sustainable Housing*, BSRIA.

- Boyle, G. (1996) *Renewable Energy Power for a Sustainable Future*, Oxford University Press.
- Roalkvam, D. (1997) *Naturlig Ventilasjon*, NABU/NFR (in Norwegian), translation from Gaia.
- Tregenza, P. and Loe, D. (1998) *The Design of Lighting*, E&FN Spon.
- Baker, N. and Steemers, K. (1999) *Energy and Environment in Architecture: a technical design guide* (LT Method 2.1), University of Cambridge.
- IEA (2000) *Things That Go Blip in the Night*, IEA Publications: www.iea. org/textbase/nppdf/free/2000/blipinthenight01.pdf
- Beggs, C.B. (2002) *Energy: management, supply and conservation*, Butterworth-Heinemann.
- TM22 (2006) *Energy Assessment and Reporting Methodology*, CIBSE.
- Halliday S.P (2007) *Sustainable Construction,* Butterworth-Heinemann, includes chapters on lighting and daylighting, ventilation and cooling, renewable energy, electrical systems and heating, with case studies.
- Building Research Establishment: www.bre.co.uk.
- BRECSU publications list for good practice case studies, guides and general information leaflets – many of which are free – covering airtightness, energy efficiency, cooling and strategic issues: www.bre. co.uk
- Carbon Trust – for ventilation, cooling and energy efficiency in buildings: www.thecarbontrust.co.uk
- Centre for Alternative Technology (CAT), *Renewable Energy Guides*: www.cat.org.uk
- Construction Information Service: http://products.ihs.com/cis/sitemap/a/a.asp
- Department of Trade and Industry – the DTI New and Renewables Programme is a source of policy guidance. The website is the source of information on contemporary policy: www.dti.gov.uk/energy/sources/ renewables/index.html
- Future Energy Solutions (formerly ETSU) – extensive publications lists are readily available on all the different technologies, including a vast record of commissioned reports, factsheets, demonstration projects and case studies, categorised under energy from waste, biomass, wind, tidal, solar, fuel cells, small-scale hydro. There are hundreds of titles: www. aea-energy-and-environment.co.uk/
- International Energy Agency, *Standby Power Use and the IEA "1-watt Plan"*: www.iea.org/textbase/subjectqueries/standby.asp
- Usable Buildings Trust: www.usablebuildings.co.uk

Planning, Transport and Urban Design

- Geddes, P. (1931) *Sciences in General*, Life.
- Mumford, L. (1961) *The City in History*, Penguin.
- McHarg, I. (1968) *Design with Nature*, MIT Press.
- Girardet, H. (1992) *The Gaia Atlas of Cities*, Gaia Books Ltd.
- Whitelegg, J. (1993) *Transport for a Sustainable Future: The Case for Europe*, Bellhaven Press.
- Liddell, H. and Mackie, A. (1994) *Energy Conservation and Planning*, Scottish Office.
- Morrison, C. and Halliday, S.P. (2000) *Working with Participation No. 5: EcoCity – A model for children's participation in the planning and regeneration of their local environment*, Children in Scotland.
- Halliday, S.P. (2007) *Sustainable Construction*, Butterworth-Heinemann, includes a chapter on urban ecology, with case studies.

Addresses and Websites

The following is a list of the websites of organisations that have a specific expertise in built environment issues and can provide information and guidance to support sustainable design.

- AECB (Association for Environment Conscious Building) – covers a wide range of expertise from architecture to specialist sub-contractors: www.aecb.net
- CABE (Commission for Architecture and the Built Environment): www.cabe.org.uk
- The Children's Parliament: www.childrensparliament.co.uk
- Communities and Local Government – Building Regulations, housing, sustainable development: www.communities.gov.uk
- DEFRA's site for environmental legislation and forthcoming EU directives, affecting sustainability: www.dti.gov.uk/construction/sustain/scb.pdf
- Department of Trade and Industry (sustainable development) – policy development and research programmes: www.sustainable-development.gov.uk
- Department of Trade and Industry (other): www.dti.gov.uk
- Environment Agency: www.environment-agency.gov.uk; including Netregs: www.netregs.gov.uk
- Environment and Heritage Service (Northern Ireland): www.ehsni.gov.uk
- Natural England: www. naturalengland.org.uk
- RIAS (Royal Incorporation of Architects in Scotland): www.rias.org.uk
- RIBA (Royal Institute of British Architects): www.riba.org.uk
- Salvo News and Salvo Guide: www.salvo.org.uk

- SEDA (Scottish Ecological Design Association): www.seda2.org
- SEPA (Scottish Environmental Protection Agency): www.sepa.org.uk
- SGR (Scientists for Global Responsibility): www.sgr.org.uk
- Sustainable Development Commission: www.sd-commission.gov.uk
- Sustrans – promotes sustainable transport through a wide range of initiatives: www.sustrans.org.uk
- Waste and Resources Action Programme: www.wrap.org.uk

Sustainable Development Journals

- *The Ecologist*: www.theecologist.org
- *New Internationalist*: www.newint.org
- *Resurgence*: www.resurgence.org
- *Ethical Consumer*: www.ethicalconsumer.org